INSIDE MLB

SAN DIEGO
PADRES

BY TODD KORTEMEIER

An Imprint of Abdo Publishing
abdobooks.com

abdobooks.com

Published by Abdo Publishing, a division of ABDO, PO Box 398166, Minneapolis, Minnesota 55439. Copyright © 2023 by Abdo Consulting Group, Inc. International copyrights reserved in all countries. No part of this book may be reproduced in any form without written permission from the publisher. SportsZone™ is a trademark and logo of Abdo Publishing.

Printed in the United States of America, North Mankato, Minnesota.
102022
012023

Cover Photo: Kyle Cooper/Colorado Rockies/Getty Images Sport/Getty Images
Interior Photos: Gregory Bull/AP Images, 4, 6; Alan Band/Fox Photos/Avalon/Hulton Archive/Getty Images, 8; Focus on Sport/Getty Images Sport/Getty Images, 9, 22; Lenny Ignelzi/AP Images, 10, 29, 35; Diamond Images/Getty Images, 12; Focus on Sport/Getty Images, 15; George Gojkovoic/Getty Images Sport/Getty Images, 17; Owen C. Shaw/Getty Images Sport/Getty Images, 18; News Base/AP Images, 21; Rich Vesely/MLB Photos/Getty Images Sport/Getty Images, 24; Larry Goren/Four Seam Images/AP Images, 27; Vincent LaForet/Allsport/Getty Images Sport/Getty Images, 31; Rich Piling/Major League Baseball/Getty Images, 32; Will Powers/AP Images, 37; Nuccio DiNuzzo/Getty Images Sport/Getty Images, 39; Thearon W. Henderson/Getty Images Sport/Getty Images, 41

Editor: Charlie Beattie
Series Designer: Joshua Olson

Library of Congress Control Number: 2022940476

Publisher's Cataloging-in-Publication Data

Names: Kortemeier, Todd, author.
Title: San Diego Padres / by Todd Kortemeier
Description: Minneapolis, Minnesota: Abdo Publishing, 2023 | Series: Inside MLB | Includes online resources and index.
Identifiers: ISBN 9781098290306 (lib. bdg.) | ISBN 9781098275501 (ebook)
Subjects: LCSH: San Diego Padres (Baseball team)--Juvenile literature. | Baseball teams--Juvenile literature. | Professional sports--Juvenile literature. | Sports franchises--Juvenile literature. | Major League Baseball (Organization)--Juvenile literature.
Classification: DDC 796.35764--dc23

TABLE OF CONTENTS

CHAPTER 1
CALIFORNIA BORN 4

CHAPTER 2
HALL OF FAME TALENT 12

CHAPTER 3
THE LONG WAY BACK 22

CHAPTER 4
KEEPING THE FAITH 32

TIMELINE 42
TEAM FACTS 44
TEAM TRIVIA 45
GLOSSARY 46
MORE INFORMATION 47
ONLINE RESOURCES 47
INDEX 48
ABOUT THE AUTHOR 48

CHAPTER 1

CALIFORNIA BORN

San Diego Padres fans had waited 14 years to see their team back in the playoffs. Now, on October 1, 2020, the long journey seemed to be ending with a thud. The Padres had already lost Game 1 of the National League (NL) wild card series to the St. Louis Cardinals. One more loss and San Diego's season would be over. And entering the bottom of the sixth inning in Game 2, St. Louis led 6–2. The Padres needed a spark.

Fernando Tatis Jr. came up with two runners on in the bottom of the sixth. On a 2–2 pitch, Tatis crushed a ball to left field. He knew it was gone right away. As Tatis strutted out of

Fernando Tatis Jr. tosses his bat away after hitting a home run against the St. Louis Cardinals during the 2020 National League wild-card series.

Wil Myers watches as his second home run of the game leaves the ballpark.

the batter's box, he tossed his bat away and shouted into the dugout to fire up his teammates.

The rest of the Padres got the message. Up next was Manny Machado. The star third baseman launched a 3–2 pitch to left-center field to tie the game. As he advanced to first, he barked more encouragement into the team dugout.

In the seventh, outfielder Wil Myers completed the comeback. He led off the inning with another home run. Four batters later, Tatis added his second of the game. The two-run shot made it 9–6. Myers also added a second homer in the eighth as the Padres held on to win 11–9. The incredible offensive display showed the rest of Major League Baseball (MLB) just how dangerous the young Padres were.

THE START OF A MISSION

San Diego has seen its share of star power on the baseball diamond. One of the biggest stars in baseball history began his career with the San Diego Padres. But they were not the Padres of today.

In 1936 a minor league team moved to San Diego from Los Angeles, where they had been called the Stars. San Diego wanted a new nickname and selected Padres. The name came from San Diego's history of Spanish colonization. The Catholic priests who started the first Spanish colonies were called *padre*, which translates to "father."

One of the first players the minor league Padres signed was a local teenage star named Ted Williams. Just one month after Williams finished his career at Herbert Hoover High School, he became a pro baseball player. In his second season, Williams whacked 23 home runs and helped the Padres capture the Pacific Coast League (PCL) championship. Just two years later, he began a Hall of Fame career in Major League Baseball with the Boston Red Sox.

The minor league Padres played their first 22 seasons at Lane Field in downtown San Diego. They then moved inland to Westgate Park in the city's Mission Valley region. The Padres won PCL titles at both parks. And huge crowds often came out to watch them.

San Diego Stadium, later known as Jack Murphy Stadium and Qualcomm Stadium, was a key factor in the Padres becoming an MLB team.

BIG-LEAGUE STRUGGLES

Padres owner C. Arnholt Smith had big dreams for the city. His enthusiasm earned him the nickname "Mr. San Diego." One of his ideas was to take his minor league team to the big leagues.

Smith got the chance in 1967. The NL was looking to expand by two teams. Smith believed San Diego was a perfect spot for a new club. A brand-new stadium helped sell others on Smith's vision. The 50,000-seat venue was being built as the home of pro football's San Diego Chargers. It also could host baseball, and the PCL Padres moved there in 1968.

The stadium turned out to be a great fit for an MLB team as well. On May 27, 1968, San Diego was officially chosen to get a new team to begin play in 1969.

Smith kept the Padres nickname. And the team adopted a logo featuring a bat-swinging Spanish priest. It was known as the Swinging Friar. He wore a brown and gold robe to fit the team's colors.

Nate Colbert's single-season Padres record of 38 home runs stood from 1970 to 1998.

MLB held an expansion draft for both the Padres and their fellow newcomers, the Montreal Expos, to build up their rosters. The draft netted San Diego key early contributors such as 21-year-old starting pitcher Clay Kirby and 23-year-old first baseman Nate Colbert. Many of the 1969 Padres were young players.

One of the team's older players was 27-year-old third baseman Ed Spiezio. He hit the team's first home run on Opening Day as San Diego beat the Houston Astros 2–1. However, only 23,000 fans were in attendance. General manager Buzzy Bavasi worried fans were staying away because they thought San Diego still had only a minor league team.

Things didn't get much better after that. The Padres won only 52 games, and attendance continued to drop.

Colbert became a three-time All-Star, and Kirby developed into a solid pitcher. But the Padres finished in last place for six straight years.

RAY SAVES THE DAY

Shortly after another 100-loss season in 1973, rumors started to swirl. The word was out that the Padres might be on their way to Washington, DC.

The nation's capital had just lost its team to Texas in 1972. Smith was losing money and looking for someone to buy the woeful Padres. On December 6, 1973, the NL approved a sale to Washington businessman Joseph Danzansky.

New uniforms were made. Baseball cards were printed showing "Washington" instead of San Diego. But the city sued Smith for breaking his lease at San Diego Stadium. Rather than fight an expensive legal battle, Smith chose to sell the team to a local owner instead.

THE FAMOUS CHICKEN

In 1974 San Diego State University student Ted Giannoulas was hired to wear a chicken suit for a radio promotion. Giannoulas had the idea to wear the suit to a Padres game to see if he could get in for free. The plan worked, and Giannoulas roamed the stands entertaining fans. The San Diego Chicken soon became a memorable part of Padres games. The mascot became so beloved that the costume now hangs in the National Baseball Hall of Fame.

Ray Kroc is most famous for building McDonald's restaurants into a worldwide chain. But Padres fans also know him as the man who saved baseball in San Diego. Kroc stepped up in 1974 to buy the Padres and keep them from moving.

When Ray Kroc bought the Padres in 1974, he hoped he could turn the team into a winner.

Just before Kroc bought the team, San Diego traded for veteran stars Willie McCovey and Matty Alou. That helped increase fan interest in 1974. That year 39,000 supporters turned up to the team's home opener. However, the Padres were routed 8–0 by the Los Angeles Dodgers. Late in the game, Kroc grabbed the stadium's public address microphone and said to the fans, "Ladies and gentlemen, I suffer with you." He then told the fans that "this was the most stupid baseball playing I've ever seen."

Kroc apologized for scolding his team in public, but not much changed. The Padres went on to lose 102 games that year. While big-league baseball was in San Diego to stay, turning the team around was not going to be easy.

CHAPTER 2

HALL OF FAME TALENT

Pitcher Randy Jones struggled right along with the rest of the Padres in 1974. He lost a major league–leading 22 games. But things were different in 1975. The team still had a poor offense, so pitching was going to be key for Jones and the rest of the staff. Jones worked hard in the offseason to improve his delivery.

With his curly blond hair bursting out from under his cap, Jones lowered his earned-run average (ERA) by more than two runs to lead the NL. Instead of losing 20 games, he won 20. He was an All-Star and finished second in Cy Young Award voting for the best pitcher in the NL.

Randy Jones's dominating sinker earned him the nickname "Junkman."

Jones then won the award in 1976. He led the majors with 22 wins and 25 complete games in his 40 starts. Jones's Cy Young Award was the first major honor for any Padre.

MORE STARS ARRIVE

The Padres improved behind Jones's amazing performances. But they were still only good enough to win 73 games. It took the addition of a few more young stars for San Diego to truly break through and compete.

Outfielder Dave Winfield was the Padres' top draft pick in 1973. An amazing all-around athlete in high school and college, Winfield was also drafted by pro football and basketball teams. But luckily for the Padres, he chose professional baseball.

Winfield was such a talented player that he skipped the minor leagues and went straight to the majors. Blessed with power and speed, his steady improvement made him an All-Star by 1977. Winfield went on to make the

FROM BOOTH TO BENCH

Jerry Coleman was a former MLB player and the Most Valuable Player (MVP) of the 1950 World Series with the New York Yankees. In 1972 he became the lead radio broadcaster for the Padres. Eight years later, he made the move out of the radio booth and onto the bench as the Padres' new manager. The Padres lost 89 games, so Coleman went right back to the press box and continued to enjoy a Hall of Fame broadcasting career.

Dave Winfield's 118 RBIs in 1979 led the major leagues and set a new Padres record.

All-Star team for the next three seasons as he grew into a Hall of Fame career.

In 1978 another future Hall of Famer broke in with the Padres. Shortstop Ozzie Smith was known as "the Wizard" for his magical defense. He wowed fans with his diving plays and hit well enough to finish runner-up for Rookie of the Year.

Ray Kroc also used his wealth to sign some top veteran players. Reliever Rollie Fingers had been a key part of three Oakland Athletics World Series championships earlier in the decade. Starting pitcher Gaylord Perry had been an American League (AL) Cy Young winner with Cleveland. After winning the NL award in 1978 with San Diego, Perry became the first pitcher to claim that honor in each league.

The Padres hosted the All-Star Game in 1978, with Winfield and Fingers getting big cheers from the home crowd. Following the All-Star break, the Padres reeled off 10 wins in a row. They went on to secure a winning record for the first time but still finished 11 games back in the NL West Division.

A GOLDEN ERA

What could have been a promising young core for the Padres did not last long. Winfield signed a 10-year deal with the New York Yankees after 1980. Smith was traded to the St. Louis Cardinals for All-Star shortstop Garry Templeton after 1981. Disappointed San Diego fans had to watch both players achieve great success elsewhere.

The Padres did their best to replace them. Veteran first baseman Steve Garvey signed in 1983. Star reliever Goose Gossage became the highest-paid pitcher in baseball when he signed with the Padres in 1984. But the biggest addition in Padres history had already joined the team in 1982.

Tony Gwynn was a star outfielder and basketball player at San Diego State University. He was drafted by the Padres

Tony Gwynn hit .289 in 54 games as a rookie in 1982 and never hit below .309 again the rest of his career.

and basketball's San Diego Clippers on the same day in 1981. Basketball was Gwynn's first love, but he chose to play baseball professionally since he was such a talented hitter.

Gwynn made his MLB debut on July 19, 1982, against the Philadelphia Phillies. He picked up two hits. Phillies star Pete Rose, who would soon become baseball's all-time hit leader, greeted Gwynn after the second hit. "Congratulations," Rose told Gwynn. "Don't catch me in one night."

Garry Templeton played more than 1,200 career games for the Padres and served as team captain for four seasons in the late 1980s.

PLAYOFF FEVER

The 1984 season began on a sad note. Kroc died on January 14, shortly after signing Gossage to his contract. Kroc's wife, Joan, took over the team. In tribute the Padres wore Kroc's initials, RAK, on their sleeves that season.

The team honored its late owner with a memorable year. Garvey led San Diego with 86 runs batted in (RBIs). Templeton was a standout shortstop. And Gwynn won his first career batting title with an average of .351.

The Padres took first place in June and never looked back. A 5–4 home victory over the San Francisco Giants on September 20 clinched San Diego's first-ever division title. That year almost 2 million fans came through the gates at Padres home games.

The Padres' NL Championship Series (NLCS) opponents were the Chicago Cubs. The series started in Chicago at Wrigley Field for two games. In Game 1, the Cubs jumped on Padres starter Eric Show and went on to win 13–0. Game 2 was closer, but it went Chicago's way. Suddenly the Padres' playoff run was almost over.

GARVEY'S MIRACLE

A packed stadium of nearly 60,000 Padres fans awaited the team in Game 3. They were quieted when the Cubs took an early 1–0 lead. But the Padres woke up, exploding for seven runs in two innings to win their first-ever playoff game 7–1.

Chicago had another chance to close out the Padres in Game 4 after San Diego let a late 5–3 lead slip away. It was still 5–5 going into the bottom of the ninth. Cubs star closer Lee Smith came on to keep the game tied.

Smith got the first out. Then he allowed a single to Gwynn. Garvey strode to the plate. The righty already had three hits on the day. He hammered Smith's 1–0 pitch to right-center field. The home crowd roared as the ball sailed over the fence. Garvey raised his fist in the air as he rounded the bases. The walk-off home run tied the best-of-five series 2–2.

The Padres' home crowd was ready for the deciding Game 5. Once again the Cubs built an early 3–0 lead. It was 3–2 when the Padres came to bat in the bottom of the seventh. With one out and a man on, San Diego's Tim Flannery hit a grounder to first base. Chicago's Leon Durham booted the ball, allowing the tying run to score. After an Alan Wiggins single, Gwynn put San Diego ahead. His double scored both runners. Gossage recorded the final outs in the ninth and was mobbed by his teammates. San Diego celebrated an incredible game and series comeback on its way to the World Series.

San Diego's magic didn't extend to the Fall Classic. Facing a Detroit Tigers team that had won 104 games during the season

Steve Garvey, *left,* **and San Diego third base coach Ozzie Virgil celebrate Garvey's walk-off home run in Game 4 of the 1984 NLCS.**

was too tough. The Padres picked up a 5–3 win in Game 2 thanks to a go-ahead three-run homer from Kurt Bevacqua in the fifth inning. But that was the lone highlight of the series. Detroit rolled to a 4–1 win. San Diego's greatest season had come up just short.

CHAPTER 3

THE LONG WAY BACK

The Padres didn't reach the playoffs again for the rest of the 1980s. But Tony Gwynn provided plenty of highlights on his own. Fans got used to seeing the lefty flick hit after hit the opposite way through the gap between the shortstop and third baseman. The team's one sure thing was that the right fielder would hit over .300. The only question was by how much. In 1987 he hit .370 to win a second batting title. His averages dipped the next two seasons, but he was still the NL's top hitter each year.

In 1989 the team was contending again. Reliever Mark Davis won the NL Cy Young Award. Catcher Benito Santiago was an

> Tony Gwynn is one of only 17 players in MLB history to play at least 20 seasons with one team.

Fred McGriff hit 84 home runs and had 256 RBIs in 2 1/2 seasons with San Diego.

All-Star. The Padres won 89 games, but that was three games behind the rival San Francisco Giants in the NL West.

The 1990 season brought big changes. For the first time since 1974, the Kroc family was no longer in charge of the Padres. TV producer Tom Werner bought the team and changed its entire identity.

Since 1969 the Padres had featured brown as their main uniform color. But the uniforms had some critics over the years, and Werner listened to them. He changed the team colors from brown and orange to blue and orange starting with the 1991 season. The blue came from the original minor league Padres.

The Padres had some stars wearing those new colors. Besides Gwynn, there were promising sluggers Fred McGriff, Gary Sheffield, and Tony Fernandez. They were known as "the Four Tops" after a musical quartet of the same name.

However, by the end of the 1993 season, San Diego had traded McGriff, Sheffield, and Fernandez. All three went on to great success elsewhere while the Padres struggled. That season the Padres lost 101 games as Werner became more and more unpopular with fans.

FLIRTING WITH .400

Despite the team's losing record, Gwynn just kept chugging along. And in 1994, "Mr. Padre" was at his best. Entering that season, his highest single-season average had been the .370 mark in 1987. The last player in baseball history to average at least .400 had been San Diego's own Ted Williams, who did so with the Boston Red Sox in 1941. Gwynn looked as if he could be next. Only twice during the season did he go back-to-back games without a hit.

Through the first 11 days of August, Gwynn was hitting .475 for the month. That brought his overall average up to .394. But on August 12, baseball shut down. The players were going on strike.

The season never resumed. The strike even wiped out the World Series. Baseball fans never got the chance to see if Gwynn could match Williams.

After the season, Werner sold the team to a new ownership group led by John Moores. The new front office was aggressive. Over the next few seasons, they added slugging third baseman Ken Caminiti, first baseman Wally Joyner, and outfielders Greg Vaughn and Steve Finley in trades. By 1996 the Padres were contenders again.

San Diego and the rival Los Angeles Dodgers dueled all year for the division title. But a September slump saw the Padres fall behind. The teams played the final series of the year against each other in Dodger Stadium.

The Padres needed to win all three games to win the West. They took the first two by 4–2 and 5–2 margins. The final

HONOR

The US military has several bases located in San Diego. The Padres wear camouflage-themed uniforms for each Sunday home game. They were also the first sports team to have an annual military appreciation game.

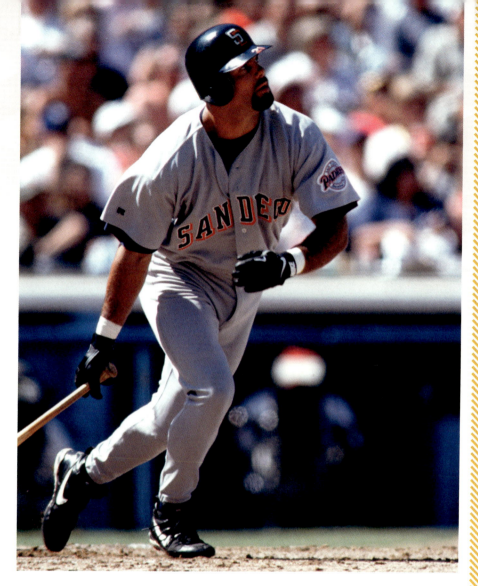

Ken Caminiti won the NL MVP, Silver Slugger, and Gold Glove Awards in 1996.

game was scoreless into the 11th inning. But Chris Gwynn, Tony's younger brother, finally broke the deadlock. His two-run double was the difference in a 2–0 win that clinched the comeback and the division.

A RUN TO REMEMBER

The 1996 season ended with a three-game sweep by the St. Louis Cardinals in the playoffs. But Caminiti was NL MVP, and Tony Gwynn won his third of four batting titles in a row. San Diego was building something special.

They hoped to build a new ballpark too. The Padres' home was aging and was designed more for football than for baseball. But the team's new owners did what they could, adding a new video board and palm trees beyond the outfield wall.

When the Padres were winning, the home crowd could bring a huge, noisy advantage. And there was plenty of noise in 1998 as the Padres got off to their best start ever. A big boost was ace righthander Kevin Brown, who led the pitching staff.

San Diego started 19–7 and was 57–31 at the All-Star break. The Padres didn't let up as they cruised to the NL West title with a team-record 98 wins. Star closer Trevor Hoffman saved 53 of them. Vaughn crushed 50 homers.

Despite the historic season, the Padres had fewer wins than any of their playoff opponents. Up first were the 102-win Houston Astros. The Padres jumped on Houston's ace, Randy Johnson, beating him twice to win the NL Division Series (NLDS) in four games.

In the NLCS, San Diego faced the 106-win Atlanta Braves. The Braves had a supercharged rotation led by future Hall of Famers Tom Glavine, John Smoltz, and Greg Maddux. But it was the Padres' pitchers who got the better of Atlanta.

A 10th-inning homer by Caminiti was the difference in a 3–2 Game 1 win. Brown shut out Atlanta in Game 2. Back in San Diego, lefty Sterling Hitchcock allowed one run in five innings as the Padres took a 3–0 series lead. Atlanta won the next two to close the gap. But Hitchcock led a shutout effort in Game 6 that sent the Padres back to the World Series.

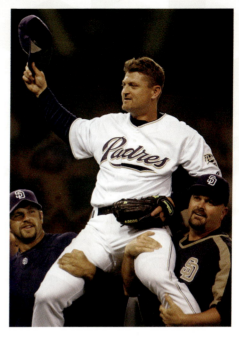

Trevor Hoffman was the first big-league closer to top both 500 and 600 saves in his career.

A GAME OF INCHES

Awaiting them in the World Series was the Padres' toughest opponent yet. The New York Yankees seemed unbeatable to many baseball experts. They had set an AL record with

114 wins. And the Padres had to start on the road in iconic Yankee Stadium.

After falling behind 2–0, the Padres battled back. Vaughn tied the game with a two-run homer in the third. Gwynn was not normally a home-run hitter, but an inning later he knocked a two-run shot off the third deck in right field to give San Diego a 4–2 lead. Vaughn followed up with a solo blast to make it 5–2 in front of a stunned New York crowd.

That lead lasted until the bottom of the seventh. New York's Chuck Knoblauch hit a three-run homer to tie the game. The Yankees then loaded the bases for slugging first baseman Tino Martinez. On a 2–2 pitch, Padres reliever Mark Langston threw a fastball that looked like a strike. Had it been called, the inning would have ended. But the pitch was called a ball. Martinez hit the next offering for a grand slam over the right-field wall. Though the Padres got a run back in the eighth inning, the game went down as a bitter 9–6 defeat.

A BALLPARK FOR SAN DIEGO

Shortly after the 1998 World Series, the Padres and their fans got a big win. Voters approved a plan to help build a new ballpark in downtown San Diego to replace the aging Qualcomm Stadium. Nearly 60 percent of voters voted yes. The ballpark was originally scheduled to open in 2002, but construction delays pushed it back until 2004.

Padres shortstop Chris Gomez, *left*, **congratulates outfielder Greg Vaughn after Vaughn's two-run homer in Game 1 of the 1998 World Series.**

San Diego never recovered. The Padres were blown out in the second game. They held a lead in Game 3 before losing a one-run game. Then they were shut out in Game 4. But even as the Yankees celebrated, Padres fans stayed to cheer for their team for giving them memories of the best season in team history.

CHAPTER 4

KEEPING THE FAITH

Much like the 1984 team, the Padres couldn't recapture their World Series glory after 1998. Many of the key players left or were traded, including Steve Finley, Ken Caminiti, and Kevin Brown. Despite a 14-game winning streak in 1999, the new-look Padres finished fourth in the NL West.

The biggest highlight of the season once again came from Tony Gwynn. On August 6, in Montreal, Gwynn lined a single to center for the 3,000th hit of his career. It was the latest achievement for one of the game's greatest hitters.

Gwynn was 39 years old in 1999. Age and bad knees were catching up to him. Over the next two seasons, he played only 107 total games. But he still managed to hit over .300

Tony Gwynn celebrates after scoring the winning run in the 1994 MLB All-Star Game. Gwynn was an All-Star 15 times during his long career with the Padres.

both years. He retired after the 2001 season having topped the .300 mark in 19 straight years. On the final day of the season, more than 60,000 fans showed up at the game to say goodbye to Mr. Padre.

HEADING DOWNTOWN

After 34 years in Mission Valley, the Padres moved south to downtown San Diego when they opened Petco Park in 2004. The new ballpark was designed just for baseball and featured all the modern perks for fans. The park was built in an old warehouse district of the city, and the team even built the park around one of the buildings. The corner of the building became Petco Park's left-field foul pole.

The Padres soon treated San Diego fans to playoff baseball in their new home. Longtime manager Bruce Bochy led a new group to the playoffs in the ballpark's second season. The team was led by the home-run hitting of right fielder Brian Giles and the pitching of young ace Jake Peavy. A year later,

TWO MILESTONES

Tony Gwynn's final game came on October 7, 2001. One of his teammates, Rickey Henderson, entered the game with 2,999 career hits. Not wanting to take the focus off Gwynn, Henderson offered to sit out. Gwynn talked Henderson out of it, and Henderson collected his 3,000th hit on first pitch he saw.

Jake Peavy led the league in ERA twice during his time with the Padres.

first baseman Adrian Gonzalez joined the Padres and had a breakout season as the team rallied for another division title. The Padres erased a four-game deficit at the start of September by finishing the season 22–9.

Both playoff runs were short, however. The Padres lost in the NLDS each year to the St. Louis Cardinals. In the two series, San Diego won only one total game.

HEARTBREAKER

The 2007 Padres spent much of the summer atop the competitive NL West. The fiery Peavy won 19 games and the NL Cy Young Award. And during the season, longtime closer Trevor Hoffman became the first MLB pitcher to pass the 500-save mark since it became an official statistic in 1969. But a late-season stumble allowed both the Arizona Diamondbacks and the Colorado Rockies to catch up.

The Dodgers won the division. San Diego had a chance to clinch the wild-card spot with two games left in the season. While playing the Milwaukee Brewers, the Padres faced a familiar name in Tony Gwynn Jr., the Padres legend's son. Hoffman had two strikes on Gwynn Jr. with two outs in the ninth inning. But the younger Gwynn hit an RBI triple to tie the game, and Milwaukee eventually won. The streaking Rockies won their game, and the two teams were tied in the standings. They needed a one-game playoff in Denver to decide the wild-card spot.

The back-and-forth game went into the 13th inning tied 6–6. A two-run homer by San Diego's Scott Hairston broke the

Padres catcher Michael Barrett, *right***, tries to collect the ball in time to tag the Colorado Rockies' Matt Holliday during the teams' 2007 one-game playoff.**

deadlock, but Colorado rallied in the bottom half of the inning. Rockies outfielder Matt Holliday tied the game with a triple. He was still on third with zero outs when Jamey Carroll hit a fly ball to right field. Giles fielded it and threw home to try to catch the tagging Holliday.

On a close play, Holliday was called safe as catcher Michael Barrett dropped the ball. But replays showed Holliday never actually touched home. It didn't matter, as Barrett never had

RIP, MR. PADRE

After retiring, Tony Gwynn returned to San Diego State, where he coached baseball for 12 seasons and became a sportscaster. In 2010 he was diagnosed with cancer. He died four years later at age 54. Gwynn's death left a huge impact on the San Diego community. Gwynn lived most of his life in the San Diego area and was beloved on and off the field. A statue bearing his nickname, "Mr. Padre," stands outside Petco Park today.

a chance to pick up the ball and tag Holliday again. The Rockies were already celebrating. The game was over, and San Diego was not part of the playoff picture.

BACK TO BROWN

After the loss to the Rockies, San Diego declined for the next decade. The team made a surprise run in 2010 but fell short of the playoffs on the final day. The second-place finish was the only time San Diego rose above third in the division during the 2010s.

Bigger changes came off the field. Another new owner, Ron Fowler, bought the team in 2012. He was the first team owner who lived in the San Diego area since Ray Kroc.

Two years later, Fowler hired A. J. Preller as the team's general manager. After initially trying to bring in veteran stars, Preller changed course and started trading for younger players.

While the team struggled on the field, the talent pool increased. One deal, involving Peavy, brought back talented shortstop Fernando Tatis Jr. By the time the top prospect

Manny Machado reached his first All-Star Game as a Padre during the 2021 season.

arrived in the majors in 2019, Preller had brought in some established veterans as well. One of them was third baseman Manny Machado. The All-Star quickly became one of San Diego's key players.

The team entered 2020 poised to start a new era. But the Padres also turned back the clock. The team went back to its original brown and gold colors. Fans had long pushed for the move.

They had also been pushing for a winner. And the 2020 Padres delivered. The season was shortened to 60 games due to the COVID-19 pandemic. But San Diego still had enough time to show up as a young, exciting team on the rise. The Padres won an NL wild-card spot with a 37–23 record.

They then set about winning the team's first playoff series since 1998. It didn't look good after the Cardinals took Game 1 of the best-of-three NL wild-card series. But San Diego's five-homer display helped the Padres rally to win Game 2 and even things up. The next day, nine San Diego pitchers combined on a four-hit shutout to close out the series. Long-suffering Padres fans took to the streets to celebrate the victory.

The Padres were swept in the NLDS by the eventual World Series–champion Los Angeles Dodgers. The next year, San Diego fell back to Earth. Despite a league-leading 42 homers from Tatis, the team stumbled out of playoff contention in the tough West Division.

The team improved significantly in 2022. And in July the Padres made another huge splash. They traded for superstar outfielder Juan Soto from the Washington Nationals. The latest exciting addition to the team's lineup helped the Padres reach the NLCS. Their run stopped there, but fans in San Diego hoped the long wait for a championship was close to ending.

Fernando Tatis Jr. led MLB with 42 home runs in 2021 and finished third in NL MVP voting.

TIMELINE

1969
The Padres play their first game in team history, a 2–1 win over the Houston Astros.

1974
The team nearly moves to Washington, DC, before local businessman Ray Kroc steps in to buy the Padres and keep them in San Diego.

1976
Randy Jones wins the first Cy Young Award in Padres history.

1978
Behind star outfielder Dave Winfield and a Cy Young season from Gaylord Perry, the Padres record their first winning season in team history.

1982
Tony Gwynn makes his MLB debut with two hits against the Philadelphia Phillies.

1984
The Padres win the NL West for the first time and make it all the way to the World Series, where they lose to the Detroit Tigers in five games.

1989
Padres reliever Mark Davis wins the NL Cy Young Award, and Gwynn wins his third consecutive NL batting title with a .336 average.

1994
Tony Gwynn's average sits at .394 ending play on August 11, but his run at .400 is halted by a players' strike that cancels the rest of the season.

1996
A sweep of the Los Angeles Dodgers in the last series of the season gives the Padres the NL West title.

1998
The Padres win a team-record 98 games and make it back to the World Series, where they're swept by the New York Yankees.

1999
Tony Gwynn records his 3,000th career hit.

2001
Gwynn plays his final game in a Padres uniform.

2004
The Padres open Petco Park in downtown San Diego.

2006
San Diego wins its second straight NL West title, a first in team history.

2016
Star pitcher Jake Peavy is traded to the Chicago White Sox for shortstop prospect Fernando Tatis Jr.

2020
Tatis leads a young Padres team back to the playoffs, and San Diego wins its first playoff series in 22 years by beating the St. Louis Cardinals in the NL wild-card series.

2022
After a mid-season trade for superstar outfielder Juan Soto, the Padres make a run to the NLCS.

TEAM FACTS

FRANCHISE HISTORY
San Diego Padres (1969–)

KEY PLAYERS
Ken Caminiti (1995–98)
Nate Colbert (1969–74)
Brian Giles (2003–09)
Adrian Gonzalez (2006–10)
Tony Gwynn (1982–2001)
Trevor Hoffman (1993–2008)
Randy Jones (1973–80)
Manny Machado (2019–)
Jake Peavy (2002–09)
Juan Soto (2022–)
Fernando Tatis Jr. (2019–)
Garry Templeton (1982–91)
Dave Winfield (1973–80)

KEY MANAGERS
Bruce Bochy (1995–2006)
Dick Williams (1982–85)

HOME STADIUMS
Qualcomm Stadium
 (1969–2003)
  Also known as:
  San Diego Stadium
   (1969–80)
  Jack Murphy Stadium
   (1981–96)
Petco Park (2004–)

TEAM TRIVIA

NO NO JOE

Entering 2021, San Diego was the only MLB team without a no-hitter in its history. That run ended on April 9, when righty Joe Musgrove no-hit the Texas Rangers in a 3–0 victory.

SLAM DIEGO

On August 17, 2020, Fernando Tatis Jr. hit a grand slam. The next day, outfielder Wil Myers hit another one. On August 19, Manny Machado hit a walk-off grand slam. And when Eric Hosmer hit another grand slam on the 20th, the Padres became the first MLB team ever to hit grand slams on four consecutive days.

INSULT TO INJURY

Late in the 2007 season, Padres outfielder Milton Bradley was arguing with umpire Mike Winters. The argument became heated, and San Diego manager Bud Black came out to hold Bradley back. Bradley's knee buckled, and he suffered torn ligaments that ended his season. Bradley was a free agent that winter, and he never played for San Diego again.

SOUTH OF THE BORDER

Being close to the border, San Diego has a strong following in Mexico. In 1996 the Padres and the New York Mets played the first regular season MLB series in the Mexican city of Monterrey. The Padres also played Opening Day of the 1999 season in Monterrey against the Colorado Rockies.

GLOSSARY

ace

A team's top pitcher.

closer

A pitcher who comes in at the end of the game to secure a win for his team.

colonization

The forceful takeover of a place by outsiders.

comeback

Going from losing a game to winning it.

contract

An agreement to play for a certain team.

draft

A system for adding new players to team rosters.

expansion

The addition of new teams to a league.

minor league

A developmental level of baseball below the major leagues.

offseason

The time between seasons.

prospect

A player in a franchise's minor league system.

rookie

A first-year player.

save

A pitching statistic awarded to a player who preserves a lead under certain conditions.

veteran

A player who has played for many years.

MORE INFORMATION

BOOKS

Flynn, Brendan. *The MLB Encyclopedia*. Minneapolis, MN: Abdo Publishing, 2022.

Gitlin, Marty. *Great Baseball Debates*. Minneapolis, MN: Abdo Publishing, 2019.

Mitchell, Bo. *Ultimate MLB Road Trip*. Minneapolis, MN: Abdo Publishing, 2019.

ONLINE RESOURCES

To learn more about the San Diego Padres, please visit **abdobooklinks.com** or scan this QR code. These links are routinely monitored and updated to provide the most current information available.

INDEX

Alou, Matty, 11
Barrett, Michael, 37
Bochy, Bruce, 34
Brown, Kevin, 28–29, 33
Caminiti, Ken, 26, 28–29, 33
Colbert, Nate, 9–10
Coleman, Jerry, 14
Davis, Mark, 23
Fernandez, Tony, 25
Fingers, Rollie, 15–16
Finley, Steve, 26, 33
Garvey, Steve, 16, 19–20
Giannoulas, Ted, 11
Giles, Brian, 34, 37
Gonzalez, Adrian, 35
Gossage, Goose, 16, 19–20
Gwynn, Chris, 27
Gwynn, Tony, 16–17, 19–20, 23, 25–26, 28, 30, 33, 34, 38
Gwynn Jr., Tony, 36
Henderson, Rickey, 34
Hitchcock, Sterling, 29
Hoffman, Trevor, 28, 36
Jones, Randy, 13–14
Joyner, Wally, 26
Kirby, Clay, 9–10
Kroc, Ray, 11, 15, 19, 38
Langston, Mark, 30
Machado, Manny, 6, 39
McCovey, Willie, 11
McGriff, Fred, 25
Myers, Wil, 6
Peavy, Jake, 34, 36, 38
Perry, Gaylord, 16
Preller, A. J., 38–39
Santiago, Benito, 23
Sheffield, Gary, 25
Show, Eric, 19
Smith, C. Arnholt, 8–10
Smith, Ozzie, 15–16
Soto, Juan, 40
Spiezio, Ed, 9
Tatis Jr., Fernando, 5–6, 38, 40
Templeton, Garry, 16, 19
Vaughn, Greg, 26, 28, 30
Williams, Ted, 7, 25–26
Winfield, Dave, 14, 16

ABOUT THE AUTHOR

Todd Kortemeier is a writer, an editor, and a lifelong San Diego Padres fan who grew up idolizing Tony Gwynn and Trevor Hoffman. He and his wife and daughter now enjoy cheering on Fernando Tatis Jr. and Manny Machado from their home near Minneapolis.